THE LORD'S PRAYER

The Lord's Prayer

© 2016 Christian Art Gifts, RSA
Christian Art Gifts Inc., IL, USA

First edition 2016

Designed by Christian Art Gifts

Images used under license from Shutterstock.com

Scripture quotations marked NIV are taken from the *Holy Bible*, New International Version® NIV®. Copyright © 1973, 1978, 1984, 2011 by International Bible Society. Used by permission of Biblica, Inc.® All rights reserved worldwide.

Scripture quotations marked ESV are taken from the *Holy Bible*, English Standard Version. Copyright © 2001 by Crossway Bibles, a division of Good News Publishers. Used by permission. All rights reserved.

Scripture quotations marked NKJV are taken from the New King James Version. Copyright © 1979, 1980, 1982 by Thomas Nelson, Inc. Used by permission. All rights reserved.

Scripture quotations marked NLT are taken from the *Holy Bible*, New Living Translation®, copyright © 1996, 2004, 2007, 2013 by Tyndale House Foundation. Used by permission of Tyndale House Publishers, Inc., Carol Stream, Illinois 60188. All rights reserved.

Printed in China

ISBN 9781-4321-1619-4

© All rights reserved. No part of this book may be reproduced in any form without permission in writing from the publisher, except in the case of brief quotations embodied in critical articles or reviews.

16 17 18 19 20 21 22 23 24 25 – 10 9 8 7 6 5 4 3 2 1

To:

Willo

From:

Sandy & Donnie

Date:

May 13, 2018

Message:

We think of you often and pray for you health and happiness.

THE LORD'S PRAYER

In this manner, therefore, pray:
Our Father in heaven,
hallowed be Your name.
Your kingdom come.
Your will be done
on earth as it is in heaven.
Give us this day our daily bread.
And forgive us our debts,
as we forgive our debtors.
And do not lead us into temptation,
but deliver us from the evil one.
For Yours is the kingdom and
the power and the glory forever.
Amen.

Matthew 6:9-13

Contents

In this manner, therefore, pray

- How should we pray 12
- God hears our prayers 16
- God answers our prayers 20

Our Father in heaven

- Our mighty Creator 26
- God's omniscience 30
- God's omnipresence 34
- God is good 38

Hallowed be Your name

- Reverence for God 44
- Holy is the Lord 48
- The power of God's name 52

Your kingdom come, Your will be done on earth as it is in heaven

- Seek God's kingdom above all else 58
- God's will for us 62

Give us this day our daily bread

- Jesus is our Bread of Life............68
- The Bible is our daily bread............72

And forgive us our debts, as we forgive our debtors

- Repent of your sins............78
- God forgives............82
- Forgive others............86

And do not lead us into temptation

- Fight between spirit and flesh 92
- Captives of sin 96
- Strength in temptation 100

But deliver us from the evil one

- He will deliver us 106
- Salvation is in Him 110
- Victory over the evil one 114

For Yours is the kingdom and the power and the glory forever.

- God's omnipotence 120
- God's glory 124

IN THIS MANNER, THEREFORE, PRAY

"When you pray, don't be like the hypocrites who love to pray publicly on street corners and in the synagogues where everyone can see them. I tell you the truth, that is all the reward they will ever get."

Matthew 6:5 NLT

"When you pray, go into your room, close the door and pray to your Father, who is unseen. Then your Father, who sees what is done in secret, will reward you."

Matthew 6:6 NIV

"When you pray, do not heap up empty phrases as the Gentiles do, for they think that they will be heard for their many words. Do not be like them, for your Father knows what you need before you ask Him."

Matthew 6:7-8 ESV

HOW SHOULD WE PRAY

Do not be anxious about anything, but in every situation, by prayer and petition, with thanksgiving, present your requests to God. And the peace of God, which transcends all understanding, will guard your hearts and your minds in Christ Jesus.

Philippians 4:6-7 NIV

Always be joyful. Never stop praying.

1 Thessalonians 5:16-17 NLT

We do not know what we ought to pray for, but the Spirit Himself intercedes for us through wordless groans. And He who searches our hearts knows the mind of the Spirit, because the Spirit intercedes for God's people in accordance with the will of God.

Romans 8:26-27 NIV

HOW SHOULD WE PRAY

Take the helmet of salvation and the sword of the Spirit, which is the word of God. And pray in the Spirit on all occasions with all kinds of prayers and requests. With this in mind, be alert and always keep on praying for all the Lord's people.

Ephesians 6:17-18 NIV

First of all, then, I urge that supplications, prayers, intercessions, and thanksgivings be made for all people, for kings and all who are in high positions, that we may lead a peaceful and quiet life, godly and dignified in every way. This is good, and it is pleasing in the sight of God our Savior, who desires all people to be saved and to come to the knowledge of the truth.

1 Timothy 2:1-4 ESV

You ask and do not receive, because you ask amiss, that you may spend it on your pleasures.

James 4:3 NKJV

Is anyone among you in trouble? Let them pray. Is anyone happy? Let them sing songs of praise. Is anyone among you sick? Let them call the elders of the church to pray over them and anoint them with oil in the name of the Lord. And the prayer offered in faith will make the sick person well; the Lord will raise them up. If they have sinned, they will be forgiven. Therefore confess your sins to each other and pray for each other so that you may be healed. The prayer of a righteous person is powerful and effective.

James 5:13-16 NIV

GOD HEARS OUR PRAYERS

This is the confidence we have in approaching God: that if we ask anything according to His will, He hears us.

1 John 5:14 NIV

"Before they call I will answer; while they are yet speaking I will hear."

Isaiah 65:24 ESV

The LORD delights in the prayers of the upright.

Proverbs 15:8 NLT

The eyes of the Lord are on the righteous and His ears are attentive to their prayer.

1 Peter 3:12 NIV

GOD HEARS OUR PRAYERS

Truly God has listened; He has attended to the voice of my prayer. Blessed be God, because He has not rejected my prayer or removed His steadfast love from me!

Psalm 66:19-20 ESV

The Lord is far from the wicked, but He hears the prayer of the righteous.

Proverbs 15:29 NIV

Give ear to my words, O Lord, consider my meditation. Give heed to the voice of my cry, my King and my God, for to You I will pray. My voice You shall hear in the morning, O Lord; in the morning I will direct it to You, and I will look up.

Psalm 5:1-3 NKJV

GOD HEARS OUR PRAYERS

"When they call on Me, I will answer; I will be with them in trouble. I will rescue and honor them."

Psalm 91:15 NLT

The LORD hears His people when they call to Him for help. He rescues them from all their troubles.

Psalm 34:17 NLT

If you will seek God earnestly and plead with the Almighty, if you are pure and upright, even now He will rouse Himself on your behalf and restore you to your prosperous state. Your beginnings will seem humble, so prosperous will your future be.

Job 8:5-7 NLT

We know that God does not listen to sinners. He listens to the godly person who does His will.

John 9:31 NIV

The LORD is near to all who call on Him, to all who call on Him in truth. He fulfills the desire of those who fear Him; He hears their cry and saves them. The LORD watches over all who love Him, but all the wicked He will destroy.

Psalm 145:18-20 NIV

"The poor and needy search for water, but there is none; their tongues are parched with thirst. But I the LORD will answer them; I, the God of Israel, will not forsake them."

Isaiah 41:17 NIV

GOD ANSWERS OUR PRAYERS

Jesus replied, "Truly I tell you, if you have faith and do not doubt, not only can you do what was done to the fig tree, but also you can say to this mountain, 'Go, throw yourself into the sea,' and it will be done. If you believe, you will receive whatever you ask for in prayer."

Matthew 21:21-22 NIV

Then Jesus said to the disciples, "Have faith in God. I tell you the truth, you can say to this mountain, 'May you be lifted up and thrown into the sea,' and it will happen. But you must really believe it will happen and have no doubt in your heart. I tell you, you can pray for anything, and if you believe that you've received it, it will be yours."

Mark 11:22-24 NLT

GOD ANSWERS OUR PRAYERS

If we know that He hears us in whatever we ask, we know that we have the requests that we have asked of Him.

1 John 5:15 ESV

"If My people who are called by My name will humble themselves, and pray and seek My face, and turn from their wicked ways, then I will hear from heaven, and will forgive their sin and heal their land."

2 Chronicles 7:14 NKJV

They cried to the LORD in their trouble, and He delivered them from their distress.

Psalm 107:28 ESV

GOD ANSWERS OUR PRAYERS

In my distress I called upon the LORD, and cried out to my God; He heard my voice from His temple, and my cry came before Him, even to His ears.

Psalm 18:6 NKJV

"If you remain in Me and My words remain in you, ask whatever you wish, and it will be done for you."

John 15:7 NIV

We will receive from Him whatever we ask because we obey Him and do the things that please Him.

1 John 3:22 NLT

GOD ANSWERS OUR PRAYERS

"Truly, truly, I say to you, whatever you ask of the Father in My name, He will give it to you. Until now you have asked nothing in My name. Ask, and you will receive, that your joy may be full."

John 16:23-24 ESV

When you call, the LORD will answer. "Yes, I am here," He will quickly reply.

Isaiah 58:9 NLT

Evening and morning and at noon I will pray, and cry aloud, and He shall hear my voice.

Psalm 55:17 NKJV

OUR FATHER IN HEAVEN

OUR MIGHTY CREATOR

You are worthy, O Lord, to receive glory and honor and power; for You created all things, and by Your will they exist and were created.

Revelation 4:11 NKJV

You alone are the LORD. You made the skies and the heavens and all the stars. You made the earth and the seas and everything in them. You preserve them all, and the angels of heaven worship You.

Nehemiah 9:6 NLT

In the beginning God created the heavens and the earth.

Genesis 1:1 NIV

"My hands have made both heaven and earth; they and everything in them are Mine. I, the LORD, have spoken! I will bless those who have humble and contrite hearts, who tremble at My word."

Isaiah 66:2 NLT

The earth is the LORD'S, and everything in it, the world, and all who live in it; for He founded it on the seas and established it on the waters.

Psalm 24:1-2 NIV

Thus says the LORD, your Redeemer, who formed you from the womb: "I am the LORD, who made all things, who alone stretched out the heavens, who spread out the earth by Myself."

Isaiah 44:24 ESV

OUR MIGHTY CREATOR

The LORD is God, and He created the heavens and earth and put everything in place. He made the world to be lived in, not to be a place of empty chaos. "I am the LORD," He says, "and there is no other."

Isaiah 45:18 NLT

Praise Him, all His angels; praise Him, all His hosts! Praise Him, sun and moon; praise Him, all you stars of light! Praise Him, you heavens of heavens, and you waters above the heavens! Let them praise the name of the LORD, for He commanded and they were created.

Psalm 148:2-5 NKJV

All the earth shall worship You and sing praises to You; they shall sing praises to Your name.

Psalm 66:4 NKJV

OUR MIGHTY CREATOR

There is one God, the Father, from whom are all things and for whom we exist, and one Lord, Jesus Christ, through whom are all things and through whom we exist.

1 Corinthians 8:6 ESV

The heavens declare the glory of God; the skies proclaim the work of His hands.

Psalm 19:1 NIV

O Lord of hosts, God of Israel, enthroned above the cherubim, You are the God, You alone, of all the kingdoms of the earth; You have made heaven and earth.

Isaiah 37:16 ESV

GOD'S OMNISCIENCE

God is greater than our hearts, and He knows everything.

1 John 3:20 NIV

Have you not known? Have you not heard? The LORD is the everlasting God, the Creator of the ends of the earth. He does not faint or grow weary; His understanding is unsearchable.

Isaiah 40:28 ESV

"Who can hide in secret places so that I cannot see them?" declares the LORD. "Do not I fill heaven and earth?" declares the LORD.

Jeremiah 23:24 NIV

GOD'S OMNISCIENCE

Who has measured the Spirit of the LORD, or what man shows Him His counsel? Whom did He consult, and who made Him understand? Who taught Him the path of justice, and taught Him knowledge, and showed Him the way of understanding? Behold, the nations are like a drop from a bucket, and are accounted as the dust on the scales; behold, He takes up the coastlands like fine dust.

Isaiah 40:13-15 ESV

How many are Your works, LORD! In wisdom You made them all; the earth is full of Your creatures. There is the sea, vast and spacious, teeming with creatures beyond number – living things both large and small.

Psalm 104:24-25 NIV

GOD'S OMNISCIENCE

Blessed be the name of God forever and ever, to whom belong wisdom and might. He changes times and seasons; He removes kings and sets up kings; He gives wisdom to the wise and knowledge to those who have understanding.

Daniel 2:20-21 ESV

You have searched me, LORD, and You know me. You know when I sit and when I rise; You perceive my thoughts from afar. Before a word is on my tongue You, LORD, know it completely. Such knowledge is too wonderful for me, too lofty for me to attain.

Psalm 139:1-2, 4, 6 NIV

God is not human, that He should lie, not a human being, that He should change His mind.

Numbers 23:19 NIV

GOD'S OMNISCIENCE

Oh, the depth of the riches both of the wisdom and knowledge of God! How unsearchable are His judgments and His ways past finding out! For of Him and through Him and to Him are all things, to whom be glory forever.

Romans 11:33, 36 NKJV

No one can know a person's thoughts except that person's own spirit, and no one can know God's thoughts except God's own Spirit.

1 Corinthians 2:11 NLT

Wisdom is with the aged, and understanding in length of days. With God are wisdom and might; He has counsel and understanding.

Job 12:12-13 ESV

GOD'S OMNIPRESENCE

God has said, "Never will I leave you; never will I forsake you."

Hebrews 13:5 NIV

I can never escape from Your Spirit! I can never get away from Your presence! If I go up to heaven, You are there; if I go down to the grave, You are there. If I ride the wings of the morning, if I dwell by the farthest oceans, even there Your hand will guide me, and Your strength will support me.

Psalm 139:7-10 NLT

"Where two or three are gathered together in My name, I am there in the midst of them."

Matthew 18:20 NKJV

GOD'S OMNIPRESENCE

His purpose was for the nations to seek after God and perhaps feel their way toward Him and find Him – though He is not far from any one of us. For in Him we live and move and exist. As some of your own poets have said, "We are His offspring."

Acts 17:27-28 NLT

The eyes of the LORD are in every place, keeping watch on the evil and the good.

Proverbs 15:3 NKJV

Before the mountains were born or You brought forth the whole world, from everlasting to everlasting You are God.

Psalm 90:2 NIV

GOD'S OMNIPRESENCE

For thus says the One who is high and lifted up, who inhabits eternity, whose name is Holy: "I dwell in the high and holy place, and also with him who is of a contrite and lowly spirit, to revive the spirit of the lowly, and to revive the heart of the contrite."

Isaiah 57:15 ESV

You have hedged me behind and before, and laid Your hand upon me.

Psalm 139:5 NKJV

The grass withers and the flowers fall, but the word of our God endures forever.

Isaiah 40:8 NIV

GOD'S OMNIPRESENCE

The Son is the image of the invisible God, the firstborn over all creation. For in Him all things were created: things in heaven and on earth, visible and invisible, whether thrones or powers or rulers or authorities; all things have been created through Him and for Him. He is before all things, and in Him all things hold together.

Colossians 1:15-17 NIV

Look, I go forward, but He is not there, and backward, but I cannot perceive Him; when He works on the left hand, I cannot behold Him; when He turns to the right hand, I cannot see Him. But He knows the way that I take; when He has tested me, I shall come forth as gold.

Job 23:8-10 NKJV

GOD IS GOOD

Give thanks to the LORD, for He is good; His love endures forever.

Psalm 107:1 NIV

You are good, and what You do is good; teach me Your decrees.

Psalm 119:68 NIV

"Why do you call Me good?" Jesus asked. "Only God is truly good."

Mark 10:18 NLT

Oh, taste and see that the LORD is good; blessed is the man who trusts in Him!

Psalm 34:8 NKJV

GOD IS GOOD

Just then a man came up to Jesus and asked, "Teacher, what good thing must I do to get eternal life?" "Why do you ask Me about what is good?" Jesus replied. "There is only One who is good. If you want to enter life, keep the commandments."

Matthew 19:16-17 NIV

His divine power has given us everything we need for a godly life through our knowledge of Him who called us by His own glory and goodness.

2 Peter 1:3 NIV

The LORD is good to everyone. He showers compassion on all His creation. All of your works will thank You, LORD, and Your faithful followers will praise You.

Psalm 145:9-10 NLT

GOD IS GOOD

Truly God is good to Israel, to such as are pure in heart.

Psalm 73:1 NKJV

For You, O Lord, are good and forgiving, abounding in steadfast love to all who call upon You.

Psalm 86:5 ESV

Every good gift and every perfect gift is from above, and comes down from the Father of lights, with whom there is no variation or shadow of turning.

James 1:17 NKJV

GOD IS GOOD

Good and upright is the LORD; therefore He instructs sinners in His ways. He guides the humble in what is right and teaches them His way.

Psalm 25:8-9 NIV

The LORD is good, a strong refuge when trouble comes. He is close to those who trust in Him.

Nahum 1:7 NLT

The LORD said, "I will cause all My goodness to pass in front of you, and I will proclaim My name, the LORD, in your presence. I will have mercy on whom I will have mercy, and I will have compassion on whom I will have compassion."

Exodus 33:19 NIV

HALLOWED BE YOUR NAME

REVERENCE FOR GOD

Since we are receiving a Kingdom that is unshakable, let us be thankful and please God by worshiping Him with holy fear and awe. For our God is a devouring fire.

Hebrews 12:28-29 NLT

Be sure to fear the LORD and serve Him faithfully with all your heart; consider what great things He has done for you.

1 Samuel 12:24 NIV

In mercy and truth atonement is provided for iniquity; and by the fear of the LORD one departs from evil.

Proverbs 16:6 NKJV

REVERENCE FOR GOD

"I tell you, My friends, do not be afraid of those who kill the body and after that can do no more. But I will show you whom you should fear: Fear Him who, after your body has been killed, has authority to throw you into hell. Yes, I tell you, fear Him."

Luke 12:4-5 NIV

From the throne came a voice saying, "Praise our God, all you His servants, you who fear Him, small and great."

Revelation 19:5 ESV

Honor all people. Love the brotherhood. Fear God.

1 Peter 2:17 NKJV

REVERENCE FOR GOD

"'Do not curse the deaf or put a stumbling block in front of the blind, but fear your God. I am the LORD.'"

Leviticus 19:14 NIV

How joyful are those who fear the LORD – all who follow His ways! You will enjoy the fruit of your labor. How joyful and prosperous you will be!

Psalm 128:1-2 NLT

Reverence for the LORD is pure, lasting forever. The laws of the LORD are true; each one is fair.

Psalm 19:9 NLT

REVERENCE FOR GOD

The fear of the LORD is the beginning of wisdom; a good understanding have all those who do His commandments. His praise endures forever.

Psalm 111:10 NKJV

The LORD takes pleasure in those who fear Him, in those who hope in His steadfast love.

Psalm 147:11 ESV

Let the whole world fear the LORD, and let everyone stand in awe of Him. For when He spoke, the world began! It appeared at His command.

Psalm 33:8-9 NLT

HOLY IS THE LORD

They were calling out to each other, "Holy, holy, holy is the LORD of Heaven's Armies! The whole earth is filled with His glory!"

Isaiah 6:3 NLT

There is no one holy like the LORD; there is no one besides You; there is no Rock like our God.

1 Samuel 2:2 NIV

For the Scriptures say, "You must be holy because I am holy."

1 Peter 1:16 NLT

"I am the LORD, your Holy One, Israel's Creator and King."

Isaiah 43:15 NLT

HOLY IS THE LORD

For thus says the High and Lofty One who inhabits eternity, whose name is Holy: "I dwell in the high and holy place, with him who has a contrite and humble spirit, to revive the spirit of the humble, and to revive the heart of the contrite ones."

Isaiah 57:15 NKJV

Who among the gods is like You, LORD? Who is like You – majestic in holiness, awesome in glory, working wonders?

Exodus 15:11 NIV

Who will not fear, O Lord, and glorify Your name? For You alone are holy. All nations will come and worship You, for Your righteous acts have been revealed.

Revelation 15:4 ESV

HOLY IS THE LORD

The LORD of Heaven's Armies will be exalted by His justice. The holiness of God will be displayed by His righteousness.

Isaiah 5:16 NLT

Exalt the LORD our God, and worship at His footstool – He is holy.

Psalm 99:5 NKJV

O God, Your ways are holy. Is there any god as mighty as You? You are the God of great wonders! You demonstrate Your awesome power among the nations.

Psalm 77:13-14 NLT

HOLY IS THE LORD

The four living creatures, each having six wings, were full of eyes around and within. And they do not rest day or night, saying: "Holy, holy, holy, Lord God Almighty, who was and is and is to come!"

Revelation 4:8 NKJV

"Give the following instructions to the entire community of Israel. You must be holy because I, the LORD your God, am holy."

Leviticus 19:2 NLT

Rejoice in the LORD, O you righteous, and give thanks to His holy name!

Psalm 97:12 ESV

THE POWER OF GOD'S NAME

Everyone who calls on the name of the LORD will be saved.

Romans 10:13 NLT

Sing to God, sing in praise of His name, extol Him who rides on the clouds; rejoice before Him – His name is the LORD.

Psalm 68:4 NIV

You were cleansed; you were made holy; you were made right with God by calling on the name of the Lord Jesus Christ and by the Spirit of our God.

1 Corinthians 6:11 NLT

THE POWER OF GOD'S NAME

There is none like You, O Lord; You are great, and Your name is great in might.

Jeremiah 10:6 ESV

The name of the Lord is a fortified tower; the righteous run to it and are safe.

Proverbs 18:10 NIV

"My name is honored by people of other nations from morning till night. All around the world they offer sweet incense and pure offerings in honor of My name. For My name is great among the nations," says the Lord of Heaven's Armies.

Malachi 1:11 NLT

THE POWER OF GOD'S NAME

"Whatever you ask in My name, this I will do, that the Father may be glorified in the Son. If you ask Me anything in My name, I will do it."

John 14:13-14 ESV

Praise the LORD. Praise the LORD, you His servants; praise the name of the LORD. Let the name of the LORD be praised, both now and forevermore. From the rising of the sun to the place where it sets, the name of the LORD is to be praised.

Psalm 113:1-3 NIV

"She will bear a Son, and you shall call His name Jesus, for He will save His people from their sins."

Matthew 1:21 ESV

THE POWER OF GOD'S NAME

"And these signs will follow those who believe: In My name they will cast out demons; they will speak with new tongues; they will take up serpents; and if they drink anything deadly, it will by no means hurt them; they will lay hands on the sick, and they will recover."

Mark 16:17-18 NKJV

Moses protested, "If I go to the people of Israel and tell them, 'The God of your ancestors has sent me to you,' they will ask me, 'What is His name?' Then what should I tell them?" God replied to Moses, "I AM WHO I AM. Say this to the people of Israel: I AM has sent me to you."

Exodus 3:13-14 NLT

YOUR KINGDOM
COME, YOUR WILL
BE DONE ON EARTH
AS IT IS IN HEAVEN

SEEK GOD'S KINGDOM ABOVE ALL ELSE

Seek the Kingdom of God above all else, and live righteously, and He will give you everything you need.

Matthew 6:33 NLT

Let the hearts of those who seek the LORD rejoice! Seek the LORD and His strength; seek His presence continually! Remember the wondrous works that He has done, His miracles and the judgments He uttered.

1 Chronicles 16:10-12 ESV

I seek You with all my heart; do not let me stray from Your commands.

Psalm 119:10 NIV

SEEK GOD'S KINGDOM ABOVE ALL ELSE

Seek the LORD your God, and you will find Him if you seek Him with all your heart and with all your soul.

Deuteronomy 4:29 NKJV

The LORD is good to those whose hope is in Him, to the one who seeks Him.

Lamentations 3:25 NIV

"Ask, and it will be given to you; seek, and you will find; knock, and it will be opened to you. For everyone who asks receives, and the one who seeks finds, and to the one who knocks it will be opened."

Matthew 7:7-8 ESV

SEEK GOD'S KINGDOM ABOVE ALL ELSE

The lions may grow weak and hungry, but those who seek the LORD lack no good thing.

Psalm 34:10 NIV

Seek the LORD while He may be found; call upon Him while He is near; let the wicked forsake his way, and the unrighteous man his thoughts; let him return to the LORD, that He may have compassion on him, and to our God, for He will abundantly pardon.

Isaiah 55:6-7 ESV

"Seek the kingdom of God, and all these things shall be added to you."

Luke 12:31 NKJV

SEEK GOD'S KINGDOM ABOVE ALL ELSE

The Lord looks down from heaven on all mankind to see if there are any who understand, any who seek God.

Psalm 14:2 NIV

Let all those who seek You rejoice and be glad in You; let such as love Your salvation say continually, "The Lord be magnified!"

Psalm 40:16 NKJV

Those who know Your name put their trust in You, for You, O Lord, have not forsaken those who seek You.

Psalm 9:10 ESV

GOD'S WILL FOR US

Be thankful in all circumstances, for this is God's will for you who belong to Christ Jesus.

1 Thessalonians 5:18 NLT

Do not be conformed to this world, but be transformed by the renewal of your mind, that by testing you may discern what is the will of God, what is good and acceptable and perfect.

Romans 12:2 ESV

"For I know the plans I have for you," declares the LORD, "plans to prosper you and not to harm you, plans to give you hope and a future. Then you will call on Me and come and pray to Me, and I will listen to you. You will seek Me and find Me when you seek Me with all your heart."

Jeremiah 29:11-13 NIV

GOD'S WILL FOR US

"This is the only work God wants from you: Believe in the One He has sent."

John 6:29 NLT

For this is the will of God, that by doing good you should put to silence the ignorance of foolish people.

1 Peter 2:15 ESV

Be filled with the Holy Spirit, singing psalms and hymns and spiritual songs among yourselves, and making music to the Lord in your hearts. And give thanks for everything to God the Father in the name of our Lord Jesus Christ.

Ephesians 5:18-20 NLT

GOD'S WILL FOR US

Look carefully then how you walk, not as unwise but as wise, making the best use of the time, because the days are evil. Therefore do not be foolish, but understand what the will of the Lord is.

Ephesians 5:15-17 ESV

Continue to work out your salvation with fear and trembling, for it is God who works in you to will and to act in order to fulfill His good purpose. Do everything without grumbling or arguing, so that you may become blameless and pure, "children of God without fault in a warped and crooked generation." Then you will shine among them like stars in the sky as you hold firmly to the Word of Life.

Philippians 2:12-16 NIV

GOD'S WILL FOR US

"For I have come down from heaven to do the will of God who sent Me, not to do My own will. And this is the will of God, that I should not lose even one of all those He has given Me, but that I should raise them up at the last day. For it is My Father's will that all who see His Son and believe in Him should have eternal life."

John 6:38-40 NLT

"Not everyone who says to Me, 'Lord, Lord,' shall enter the kingdom of heaven, but he who does the will of My Father in heaven."

Matthew 7:21 NKJV

God's will is for you to be holy, so stay away from all sexual sin. Then each of you will control his own body and live in holiness and honor.

1 Thessalonians 4:3-4 NLT

GIVE US THIS DAY OUR DAILY BREAD

JESUS IS OUR BREAD OF LIFE

Jesus replied, "I am the Bread of Life. Whoever comes to Me will never be hungry again. Whoever believes in Me will never be thirsty."

John 6:35 NLT

"This is the bread that comes down from heaven, so that one may eat of it and not die. I am the living bread that came down from heaven. If anyone eats of this bread, he will live forever. And the bread that I will give for the life of the world is My flesh."

John 6:50-51 ESV

"Everyone who lives in Me and believes in Me will never ever die."

John 11:26 NLT

JESUS IS OUR BREAD OF LIFE

"Truly, truly, I say to you, unless you eat the flesh of the Son of Man and drink His blood, you have no life in you. Whoever feeds on My flesh and drinks My blood has eternal life, and I will raise him up on the last day. For My flesh is true food, and My blood is true drink."

John 6:53-55 ESV

"Whoever eats My flesh and drinks My blood remains in Me, and I in them. Just as the living Father sent Me and I live because of the Father, so the one who feeds on Me will live because of Me."

John 6:56-57 NIV

"Truly, truly, I say to you, whoever believes has eternal life."

John 6:47 ESV

JESUS IS OUR BREAD OF LIFE

"For God so loved the world that He gave His only begotten Son, that whoever believes in Him should not perish but have everlasting life."

John 3:16 NKJV

God gave us eternal life, and this life is in His Son. Whoever has the Son has life; whoever does not have the Son of God does not have life.

1 John 5:11-12 ESV

For the wages of sin is death, but the free gift of God is eternal life through Christ Jesus our Lord.

Romans 6:23 NLT

JESUS IS OUR BREAD OF LIFE

You make known to me the path of life; You will fill me with joy in Your presence, with eternal pleasures at Your right hand.

Psalm 16:11 NIV

"I am the true bread that came down from heaven. Anyone who eats this bread will not die as your ancestors did (even though they ate the manna) but will live forever."

John 6:58 NLT

Jesus answered, "Very truly I tell you, you are looking for Me, not because you saw the signs I performed but because you ate the loaves and had your fill. Do not work for food that spoils, but for food that endures to eternal life, which the Son of Man will give you. For on Him God the Father has placed His seal of approval."

John 6:26-27 NIV

THE BIBLE IS OUR DAILY BREAD

"You will know the truth, and the truth will set you free."

John 8:32 NIV

Your Word is a lamp to guide my feet and a light for my path.

Psalm 119:105 NLT

"Heaven and earth will pass away, but My words will never pass away."

Matthew 24:35 NIV

Jesus answered, "It is written: 'Man shall not live on bread alone, but on every word that comes from the mouth of God.'"

Matthew 4:4 NIV

THE BIBLE IS OUR DAILY BREAD

All Scripture is inspired by God and is useful to teach us what is true and to make us realize what is wrong in our lives. It corrects us when we are wrong and teaches us to do what is right.

2 Timothy 3:16 NLT

For the word of God is living and powerful, and sharper than any two-edged sword, piercing even to the division of soul and spirit, and of joints and marrow, and is a discerner of the thoughts and intents of the heart.

Hebrews 4:12 NKJV

Open my eyes, that I may see wondrous things from Your law. I am a stranger in the earth; do not hide Your commandments from me.

Psalm 119:18-19 NKJV

THE BIBLE IS OUR DAILY BREAD

Study this Book of Instruction continually. Meditate on it day and night so you will be sure to obey everything written in it. Only then will you prosper and succeed in all you do.

Joshua 1:8 NLT

In the beginning was the Word, and the Word was with God, and the Word was God. He was in the beginning with God. All things were made through Him, and without Him was not any thing made that was made.

John 1:1-3 ESV

Blessed are those whose ways are blameless, who walk according to the law of the LORD. Blessed are those who keep His statutes and seek Him with all their heart – they do no wrong but follow His ways.

Psalm 119:1-3 NIV

THE BIBLE IS OUR DAILY BREAD

Everything that was written in the past was written to teach us, so that through the endurance taught in the Scriptures and the encouragement they provide we might have hope.

Romans 15:4 NIV

Blessed is the one who does not walk in step with the wicked or stand in the way that sinners take or sit in the company of mockers, but whose delight is in the law of the Lord, and who meditates on His law day and night. That person is like a tree planted by streams of water, which yields its fruit in season and whose leaf does not wither – whatever they do prospers.

Psalm 1:1-3 NIV

AND FORGIVE
US OUR DEBTS,
AS WE FORGIVE
OUR DEBTORS

REPENT OF YOUR SINS

If we confess our sins, He is faithful and just to forgive us our sins and to cleanse us from all unrighteousness.

1 John 1:9 NKJV

Repent, then, and turn to God, so that your sins may be wiped out, that times of refreshing may come from the Lord, and that He may send the Messiah, who has been appointed for you – even Jesus.

Acts 3:19-20 NIV

The Lord is not slow to fulfill His promise as some count slowness, but is patient toward you, not wishing that any should perish, but that all should reach repentance.

2 Peter 3:9 ESV

REPENT OF YOUR SINS

People who conceal their sins will not prosper, but if they confess and turn from them, they will receive mercy.

Proverbs 28:13 NLT

Repent and be baptized every one of you in the name of Jesus Christ for the forgiveness of your sins, and you will receive the gift of the Holy Spirit.

Acts 2:38 ESV

"Repent of your sins and turn to God, for the Kingdom of Heaven is near."

Matthew 3:2 NLT

REPENT OF YOUR SINS

"But if a wicked person turns away from all his sins that he has committed and keeps all My statutes and does what is just and right, he shall surely live; he shall not die. None of the transgressions that he has committed shall be remembered against him; for the righteousness that he has done he shall live."

Ezekiel 18:21-22 ESV

"Those whom I love I rebuke and discipline. So be earnest and repent."

Revelation 3:19 NIV

From that time Jesus began to preach and to say, "Repent, for the kingdom of heaven is at hand."

Matthew 4:17 NKJV

REPENT OF YOUR SINS

Jesus answered them, "Healthy people don't need a doctor – sick people do. I have come to call not those who think they are righteous, but those who know they are sinners and need to repent."

Luke 5:31-32 NLT

"Those who are well have no need of a physician, but those who are sick. But go and learn what this means: 'I desire mercy and not sacrifice.' For I did not come to call the righteous, but sinners, to repentance."

Matthew 9:12-13 NKJV

"Go back to what you heard and believed at first; hold to it firmly. Repent and turn to Me again. If you don't wake up, I will come to you suddenly, as unexpected as a thief."

Revelation 3:3 NLT

GOD FORGIVES

"I have blotted out, like a thick cloud, your transgressions, and like a cloud, your sins. Return to Me, for I have redeemed you."

Isaiah 44:22 NKJV

As far as the east is from the west, so far has He removed our transgressions from us.

Psalm 103:12 NIV

"I will forgive their wickedness, and I will never again remember their sins."

Hebrews 8:12 NLT

The Lord our God is merciful and forgiving.

Daniel 9:9 NLT

GOD FORGIVES

Though your sins are like scarlet, they shall be as white as snow; though they are red as crimson, they shall be like wool.

Isaiah 1:18 NIV

He took a cup, and when He had given thanks He gave it to them, saying, "Drink of it, all of you, for this is My blood of the covenant, which is poured out for many for the forgiveness of sins."

Matthew 26:27-28 ESV

All the prophets testify about Him that everyone who believes in Him receives forgiveness of sins through His name.

Acts 10:43 NIV

GOD FORGIVES

Now there is no condemnation for those who belong to Christ Jesus. And because you belong to Him, the power of the life-giving Spirit has freed you from the power of sin that leads to death.

Romans 8:1-2 NLT

If anyone sins, we have an Advocate with the Father, Jesus Christ the righteous. And He Himself is the propitiation for our sins, and not for ours only but also for the whole world.

1 John 2:1-2 NKJV

We praise God for the glorious grace He has poured out on us who belong to His dear Son. He is so rich in kindness and grace that He purchased our freedom with the blood of His Son and forgave our sins.

Ephesians 1:6-7 NLT

GOD FORGIVES

He has delivered us from the domain of darkness and transferred us to the kingdom of His beloved Son, in whom we have redemption, the forgiveness of sins.

Colossians 1:13-14 ESV

Who is a God like You, who pardons sin and forgives the transgression of the remnant of His inheritance? You do not stay angry forever but delight to show mercy. You will again have compassion on us; You will tread our sins underfoot and hurl all our iniquities into the depths of the sea.

Micah 7:18-19 NIV

FORGIVE OTHERS

"When you stand praying, if you hold anything against anyone, forgive them, so that your Father in heaven may forgive you your sins."

Mark 11:25 NIV

Be kind to one another, tenderhearted, forgiving one another, as God in Christ forgave you.

Ephesians 4:32 ESV

"If you forgive those who sin against you, your heavenly Father will forgive you. But if you refuse to forgive others, your Father will not forgive your sins."

Matthew 6:14-15 NLT

FORGIVE OTHERS

Confess your sins to each other and pray for each other so that you may be healed.

James 5:16 NIV

"Do not judge, and you will not be judged. Do not condemn, and you will not be condemned. Forgive, and you will be forgiven."

Luke 6:37 NIV

"If another believer sins, rebuke that person; then if there is repentance, forgive. Even if that person wrongs you seven times a day and each time turns again and asks forgiveness, you must forgive."

Luke 17:3-4 NLT

FORGIVE OTHERS

"Then his master summoned him and said to him, 'You wicked servant! I forgave you all that debt because you pleaded with me. And should not you have had mercy on your fellow servant, as I had mercy on you?' And in anger his master delivered him to the jailers, until he should pay all his debt. So also My heavenly Father will do to every one of you, if you do not forgive your brother from your heart."

Matthew 18:32-35 ESV

"In the same way you judge others, you will be judged, and with the measure you use, it will be measured to you."

Matthew 7:2 NIV

As the Lord has forgiven you, so you also must forgive.

Colossians 3:13 ESV

FORGIVE OTHERS

Then Peter came to Him and asked, "Lord, how often should I forgive someone who sins against me? Seven times?" "No, not seven times," Jesus replied, "but seventy times seven!"

Matthew 18:21-22 NLT

"If you forgive anyone's sins, their sins are forgiven; if you do not forgive them, they are not forgiven."

John 20:23 NIV

"Forgive us our sins, for we also forgive everyone who is indebted to us. And do not lead us into temptation, but deliver us from the evil one."

Luke 11:4 NKJV

AND DO NOT LEAD US INTO TEMPTATION

FIGHT BETWEEN SPIRIT AND FLESH

The law of Moses was unable to save us because of the weakness of our sinful nature. So God did what the law could not do. He sent His own Son in a body like the bodies we sinners have. And in that body God declared an end to sin's control over us by giving His Son as a sacrifice for our sins. He did this so that the just requirement of the law would be fully satisfied for us, who no longer follow our sinful nature but instead follow the Spirit.

Romans 8:3-4 NLT

Those who live according to the flesh have their minds set on what the flesh desires; but those who live in accordance with the Spirit have their minds set on what the Spirit desires.

Romans 8:5 NIV

FIGHT BETWEEN SPIRIT AND FLESH

To be carnally minded is death, but to be spiritually minded is life and peace. Because the carnal mind is enmity against God; for it is not subject to the law of God, nor indeed can be. So then, those who are in the flesh cannot please God. But you are not in the flesh but in the Spirit, if indeed the Spirit of God dwells in you. Now if anyone does not have the Spirit of Christ, he is not His.

Romans 8:6-9 NKJV

If Christ is in you, although the body is dead because of sin, the Spirit is life because of righteousness. If the Spirit of Him who raised Jesus from the dead dwells in you, He who raised Christ Jesus from the dead will also give life to your mortal bodies through His Spirit who dwells in you.

Romans 8:10-11 ESV

FIGHT BETWEEN SPIRIT AND FLESH

If you live according to the flesh you will die; but if by the Spirit you put to death the deeds of the body, you will live.

Romans 8:13 NKJV

You, my brothers and sisters, were called to be free. But do not use your freedom to indulge the flesh; rather, serve one another humbly in love.

Galatians 5:13 NIV

Walk by the Spirit, and you will not gratify the desires of the flesh. For the desires of the flesh are against the Spirit, and the desires of the Spirit are against the flesh, for these are opposed to each other, to keep you from doing the things you want to do.

Galatians 5:16-17 ESV

FIGHT BETWEEN SPIRIT AND FLESH

But the fruit of the Spirit is love, joy, peace, forbearance, kindness, goodness, faithfulness, gentleness and self-control. Against such things there is no law.

Galatians 5:22-23 NIV

Those who belong to Christ Jesus have nailed the passions and desires of their sinful nature to His cross and crucified them there. Since we are living by the Spirit, let us follow the Spirit's leading in every part of our lives.

Galatians 5:24-25 NLT

Set your minds on things that are above, not on things that are on earth. For you have died, and your life is hidden with Christ in God.

Colossians 3:2-3 ESV

CAPTIVES OF SIN

Jesus replied, "Very truly I tell you, everyone who sins is a slave to sin. Now a slave has no permanent place in the family, but a son belongs to it forever. So if the Son sets you free, you will be free indeed."

John 8:34-36 NIV

We are all infected and impure with sin. When we display our righteous deeds, they are nothing but filthy rags. Like autumn leaves, we wither and fall, and our sins sweep us away like the wind.

Isaiah 64:6 NLT

Surely there is not a righteous man on earth who does good and never sins.

Ecclesiastes 7:20 ESV

CAPTIVES OF SIN

There is no difference between Jew and Gentile, for all have sinned and fall short of the glory of God, and all are justified freely by His grace through the redemption that came by Christ Jesus.

Romans 3:22-24 NIV

Do you not know that if you present yourselves to anyone as obedient slaves, you are slaves of the one whom you obey, either of sin, which leads to death, or of obedience, which leads to righteousness? But thanks be to God, that you who were once slaves of sin have become obedient from the heart to the standard of teaching to which you were committed, and, having been set free from sin, have become slaves of righteousness.

Romans 6:16-18 ESV

CAPTIVES OF SIN

If we claim we have not sinned, we are calling God a liar and showing that His word has no place in our hearts.

1 John 1:10 NLT

Behold, I was brought forth in iniquity, and in sin my mother conceived me.

Psalm 51:5 NKJV

When people escape from the wickedness of the world by knowing our Lord and Savior Jesus Christ and then get tangled up and enslaved by sin again, they are worse off than before.

2 Peter 2:20 NLT

CAPTIVES OF SIN

There is no one who does not sin.

1 Kings 8:46 NIV

"The Spirit of the Sovereign Lord is upon Me, for the Lord has anointed Me to bring good news to the poor. He has sent Me to comfort the brokenhearted and to proclaim that captives will be released and prisoners will be freed."

Isaiah 61:1 NLT

The Lord looked down from His sanctuary on high, from heaven He viewed the earth, to hear the groans of the prisoners and release those condemned to death.

Psalm 102:19-20 NIV

STRENGTH IN TEMPTATION

No temptation has overtaken you that is not common to man. God is faithful, and He will not let you be tempted beyond your ability, but with the temptation He will also provide the way of escape, that you may be able to endure it.

1 Corinthians 10:13 ESV

God blesses those who patiently endure testing and temptation. Afterward they will receive the crown of life that God has promised to those who love Him. And remember, when you are being tempted, do not say, "God is tempting me." God is never tempted to do wrong, and He never tempts anyone else. Temptation comes from our own desires, which entice us and drag us away.

James 1:12-14 NLT

STRENGTH IN TEMPTATION

Because He Himself suffered when He was tempted, He is able to help those who are being tempted.

Hebrews 2:18 NIV

Submit to God. Resist the devil and he will flee from you.

James 4:7 NKJV

Be strong in the Lord and in His mighty power. Put on all of God's armor so that you will be able to stand firm against all strategies of the devil. For we are not fighting against flesh-and-blood enemies, but against evil rulers and authorities of the unseen world, against mighty powers in this dark world, and against evil spirits in the heavenly places.

Ephesians 6:10-12 NLT

STRENGTH IN TEMPTATION

Stand firm then, with the belt of truth buckled around your waist, with the breastplate of righteousness in place, and with your feet fitted with the readiness that comes from the gospel of peace. In addition to all this, take up the shield of faith, with which you can extinguish all the flaming arrows of the evil one.

Ephesians 6:14-16 NIV

Since then we have a great High Priest who has passed through the heavens, Jesus, the Son of God, let us hold fast our confession. For we do not have a High Priest who is unable to sympathize with our weaknesses, but One who in every respect has been tempted as we are, yet without sin. Let us then with confidence draw near to the throne of grace, that we may receive mercy and find grace to help in time of need.

Hebrews 4:14-16 ESV

STRENGTH IN TEMPTATION

Your word I have hidden in my heart, that I might not sin against You.

Psalm 119:11 NKJV

Be alert and of sober mind. Your enemy the devil prowls around like a roaring lion looking for someone to devour. Resist him, standing firm in the faith, because you know that the family of believers throughout the world is undergoing the same kind of sufferings.

1 Peter 5:8-9 NIV

In His kindness God called you to share in His eternal glory by means of Christ Jesus. So after you have suffered a little while, He will restore, support, and strengthen you, and He will place you on a firm foundation. All power to Him forever!

1 Peter 5:10-11 NLT

BUT DELIVER
US FROM THE
EVIL ONE

HE WILL DELIVER US

Then they cried out to the LORD in their trouble, and He delivered them from their distress.

Psalm 107:6 NIV

The LORD is my rock and my fortress and my deliverer, my God, my rock, in whom I take refuge, my shield, and the horn of my salvation, my stronghold and my refuge, my Savior;
You save me from violence.

2 Samuel 22:2-3 ESV

For freedom Christ has set us free; stand firm therefore, and do not submit again to a yoke of slavery.

Galatians 5:1 ESV

HE WILL DELIVER US

I sought the LORD, and He answered me;
He delivered me from all my fears.

Psalm 34:4 NIV

"Call upon Me in the day of trouble; I will deliver you, and you shall glorify Me."

Psalm 50:15 NKJV

If you make the LORD your refuge, if you make the Most High your shelter, no evil will conquer you; no plague will come near your home. For He will order His angels to protect you wherever you go. The LORD says, "I will rescue those who love Me. I will protect those who trust in My name."

Psalm 91:9-11, 14 NLT

HE WILL DELIVER US

"Do not be afraid, for I am with you and will rescue you," declares the LORD.

Jeremiah 1:8 NIV

The LORD is my rock and my fortress and my deliverer; my God, my strength, in whom I will trust; my shield and the horn of my salvation, my stronghold. I will call upon the LORD, who is worthy to be praised; so shall I be saved from my enemies.

Psalm 18:2-3 NKJV

We can confidently say, "The Lord is my helper; I will not fear; what can man do to me?"

Hebrews 13:6-7 ESV

HE WILL DELIVER US

For in my inner being I delight in God's law; but I see another law at work in me, waging war against the law of my mind and making me a prisoner of the law of sin at work within me. What a wretched man I am! Who will rescue me from this body that is subject to death? Thanks be to God, who delivers me through Jesus Christ our Lord!

Romans 7:22-25 NIV

"Do not be afraid, for I have ransomed you. I have called you by name; you are Mine. When you go through deep waters, I will be with you. When you go through rivers of difficulty, you will not drown. When you walk through the fire of oppression, you will not be burned up; the flames will not consume you. For I am the LORD, your God, the Holy One of Israel, your Savior."

Isaiah 43:1-3 NLT

SALVATION IS IN HIM

Praise the Lord; praise God our Savior! For each day He carries us in His arms. Our God is a God who saves! The Sovereign LORD rescues us from death.

Psalm 68:19-20 NLT

Believe in the Lord Jesus, and you will be saved – you and your household.

Acts 16:31 NIV

The LORD takes pleasure in His people; He will beautify the humble with salvation.

Psalm 149:4 NKJV

SALVATION IS IN HIM

Restore to me the joy of Your salvation and grant me a willing spirit, to sustain me.

Psalm 51:12 NIV

Oh, sing to the LORD a new song! Sing to the LORD, all the earth. Sing to the LORD, bless His name; proclaim the good news of His salvation from day to day. Declare His glory among the nations, His wonders among all peoples.

Psalm 96:1-3 NKJV

It is good that one should wait quietly for the salvation of the LORD.

Lamentations 3:26 ESV

SALVATION IS IN HIM

I delight greatly in the LORD; my soul rejoices in my God. For He has clothed me with garments of salvation and arrayed me in a robe of His righteousness, as a bridegroom adorns his head like a priest, and as a bride adorns herself with her jewels. For as the soil makes the sprout come up and a garden causes seeds to grow, so the Sovereign LORD will make righteousness and praise spring up before all nations.

Isaiah 61:10-11 NIV

Jesus is the one referred to in the Scriptures, where it says, "The stone that you builders rejected has now become the cornerstone." There is salvation in no one else! God has given no other name under heaven by which we must be saved.

Acts 4:11-12 NLT

SALVATION IS IN HIM

"I am the gate; whoever enters through Me will be saved. They will come in and go out, and find pasture. The thief comes only to steal and kill and destroy; I have come that they may have life, and have it to the full. I am the good shepherd. The good shepherd lays down His life for the sheep."

John 10:9-11 NIV

God saved you by His grace when you believed. And you can't take credit for this; it is a gift from God. Salvation is not a reward for the good things we have done, so none of us can boast about it.

Ephesians 2:8-9 NLT

VICTORY OVER THE EVIL ONE

The sting of death is sin, and the power of sin is the law. But thanks be to God! He gives us the victory through our Lord Jesus Christ.

1 Corinthians 15:56-57 NIV

If God is for us, who can ever be against us? Since He did not spare even His own Son but gave Him up for us all, won't He also give us everything else?

Romans 8:31-32 NLT

Thanks be to God who always leads us in triumph in Christ, and through us diffuses the fragrance of His knowledge in every place. For we are to God the fragrance of Christ among those who are being saved and among those who are perishing.

2 Corinthians 2:14-15 NKJV

VICTORY OVER THE EVIL ONE

We know that God's children do not make a practice of sinning, for God's Son holds them securely, and the evil one cannot touch them.

1 John 5:18 NLT

The great dragon was hurled down – that ancient serpent called the devil, or Satan, who leads the whole world astray. He was hurled to the earth, and his angels with him.

Revelation 12:9 NIV

"My prayer is not that You take them out of the world but that You protect them from the evil one. They are not of the world, even as I am not of it."

John 17:15-16 NIV

VICTORY OVER THE EVIL ONE

I can do all things through Christ who strengthens me.

Philippians 4:13 NKJV

This is what the LORD says to you: "Do not be afraid or discouraged because of this vast army. For the battle is not yours, but God's."

2 Chronicles 20:15 NIV

God's way is perfect. All the LORD's promises prove true. He is a shield for all who look to Him for protection. For who is God except the LORD? Who but our God is a solid rock? God arms me with strength, and He makes my way perfect. He makes me as surefooted as a deer, enabling me to stand on mountain heights.

Psalm 18:30-33 NLT

VICTORY OVER THE EVIL ONE

Put on the full armor of God, so that you can take your stand against the devil's schemes. For our struggle is not against flesh and blood, but against the rulers, against the authorities, against the powers of this dark world and against the spiritual forces of evil in the heavenly realms.

Ephesians 6:11-12 NIV

Pray, too, that we will be rescued from wicked and evil people, for not everyone is a believer. But the Lord is faithful; He will strengthen you and guard you from the evil one.

2 Thessalonians 3:2-3 NLT

FOR YOURS IS THE
KINGDOM AND THE
POWER AND THE
GLORY FOREVER.

GOD'S OMNIPOTENCE

For ever since the world was created, people have seen the earth and sky. Through everything God made, they can clearly see His invisible qualities – His eternal power and divine nature.

Romans 1:20 NLT

He determines the number of the stars; He gives to all of them their names. Great is our Lord, and abundant in power; His understanding is beyond measure.

Psalm 147:4-5 ESV

"Humanly speaking, it is impossible. But with God everything is possible."

Matthew 19:26 NLT

GOD'S OMNIPOTENCE

"I am the Lord, the God of all mankind. Is anything too hard for Me?"

Jeremiah 32:27 NIV

We cannot imagine the power of the Almighty; but even though He is just and righteous, He does not destroy us.

Job 37:23 NLT

I know that You can do all things, and that no purpose of Yours can be thwarted.

Job 42:2 ESV

"From ancient days I am He. No one can deliver out of My hand. When I act, who can reverse it?"

Isaiah 43:13 NIV

GOD'S OMNIPOTENCE

I pray that you will understand the incredible greatness of God's power for us who believe Him. This is the same mighty power that raised Christ from the dead and seated Him in the place of honor at God's right hand in the heavenly realms. Now He is far above any ruler or authority or power or leader or anything else – not only in this world but also in the world to come. God has put all things under the authority of Christ and has made Him head over all things for the benefit of the church.

Ephesians 1:19-22 NLT

Yours, LORD, is the greatness and the power and the glory and the majesty and the splendor, for everything in heaven and earth is Yours. Yours, LORD, is the Kingdom; You are exalted as head over all.

1 Chronicles 29:11 NIV

GOD'S OMNIPOTENCE

I heard what seemed to be the voice of a great multitude, like the roar of many waters and like the sound of mighty peals of thunder, crying out, "Hallelujah! For the Lord our God the Almighty reigns."

Revelation 19:6 ESV

God sits above the circle of the earth. The people below seem like grasshoppers to Him! He spreads out the heavens like a curtain and makes His tent from them. He judges the great people of the world and brings them all to nothing. They hardly get started, barely taking root, when He blows on them and they wither. The wind carries them off like chaff.

Isaiah 40:22-24 NLT

GOD'S GLORY

Open up, ancient gates! Open up, ancient doors, and let the King of glory enter. Who is the King of glory? The LORD, strong and mighty; the LORD, invincible in battle.

Psalm 24:7-8 NLT

The Son is the radiance of God's glory and the exact representation of His being, sustaining all things by His powerful word. After He had provided purification for sins, He sat down at the right hand of the Majesty in heaven.

Hebrews 1:3 NIV

Blessed be His glorious name forever; may the whole earth be filled with His glory!

Psalm 72:19 ESV

GOD'S GLORY

His splendor was like the sunrise; rays flashed from His hand, where His power was hidden.

Habakkuk 3:4 NIV

Surely the LORD our God has shown us His glory and His greatness, and we have heard His voice from the midst of the fire. We have seen this day that God speaks with man; yet he still lives.

Deuteronomy 5:24 NKJV

The voice of the LORD is over the waters; the God of glory thunders, the LORD thunders over the mighty waters.

Psalm 29:3 NIV

GOD'S GLORY

Therefore God has highly exalted Him and bestowed on Him the name that is above every name, so that at the name of Jesus every knee should bow, in heaven and on earth and under the earth, and every tongue confess that Jesus Christ is Lord, to the glory of God the Father.

Philippians 2:9-11 ESV

For of Him and through Him and to Him are all things, to whom be glory forever.

Romans 11:36 NKJV

The earth will be filled with the knowledge of the glory of the LORD as the waters cover the sea.

Habakkuk 2:14 NIV

GOD'S GLORY

The Word became flesh and dwelt among us, and we beheld His glory, the glory as of the only begotten of the Father, full of grace and truth.

John 1:14 NKJV

"No longer will you need the sun to shine by day, nor the moon to give its light by night, for the LORD your God will be your everlasting light, and your God will be your glory."

Isaiah 60:19 NLT

We all, who with unveiled faces contemplate the Lord's glory, are being transformed into His image with ever-increasing glory, which comes from the Lord, who is the Spirit.

2 Corinthians 3:18 NIV

Amen.